THE STORY OF DRAGONS AND OTHER MONSTERS

OTHER BOOKS BY THE AUTHOR

The Alchemists: Magic Into Science
Astrology and Foretelling the Future
Cars, Boats, Trains, and Planes
    of Today and Tomorrow
ESP
Geological Disasters:
    Earthquakes and Volcanoes
Graphology
Into the Mammal's World
It Works Like This
Monsters from the Movies
Movie Monsters
Mysteries from the Past
Palmistry
Science at the Ball Game
Science Update 77
Science Update 78
The Search for Life
Servants of the Devil
The Story of Vampires
The Story of Werewolves
The Story of Witches
Teaching for Thinking
This Vital Air, This Vital Water
Traveling Into Tomorrow
Understanding Body Talk
Vampires and Other Ghosts
Werewolves and Other Monsters
Who's Out There?
The World of Microbes

THE STORY OF Dragons

AND OTHER MONSTERS

THOMAS G. AYLESWORTH
Illustrated with photographs and old prints

McGRAW-HILL BOOK COMPANY
New York • San Francisco • St. Louis • Montreal • Toronto

A Charlotte Gilbert:
La señorita de los ojos azules,
amante de libros,
y mi querida amiga.

Library of Congress Cataloging in Publication Data
Aylesworth, Thomas G   The story of dragons and other monsters.
   Bibliography: p.   Includes index.
   SUMMARY: Discusses the dragon, kraken, basilisk, mermaid, and harpy.
   1. Monsters—Juvenile literature. [1. Monsters] I. Title.
GR825.A93   398.2'1   79-21550
ISBN 0-07-002646-7

123456789 RABP 876543210

TABLE OF CONTENTS

	IN THE BEGINNING	1
1	OLD TIME DRAGONS	7
2	DRAGONS IN THE WESTERN WORLD	20
3	DRAGONS IN THE EASTERN WORLD	33
4	MONSTERS ON THE LAND	37
5	MONSTERS IN THE AIR	57
6	MONSTERS IN THE WATER	70
	AT THE END	84
	OTHER BOOKS ABOUT MONSTERS	86
	INDEX	88

Sailors, it seems, have always been believers in monsters.
Can you blame this one for saying a little prayer? This
engraving was made more than one hundred years ago.

IN THE BEGINNING

It seems as though monsters have always been with us. Stories of them, particularly of dragons, the leviathan, basilisks, and unicorns, appear in the Bible. They were described by such learned men as Aristotle, the great Greek philosopher, and Pliny the Elder, the influential Roman author.

For centuries, pressure was put on people to believe in monsters. Because of the appearances of the creatures in the Bible, disbelievers could be accused of being antireligious. And, because of the monsters mentioned in Aristotle's scientific writings and Pliny's book, *Historia Naturalis* (or *Natural History*), the doubter could also be accused of being anti-intellectual.

Alexander the Great, the conquering emperor of Macedonia in the fourth century B.C., was said to have come across many monsters in his travels. According to one historian, Alexander wrote of them. This is almost certainly a false report, but still interesting. Here is what the mighty ruler is alleged to have said: "We came to a wood inhabited by wild men with faces like ravens. We arrived at the country of the people whose feet are twisted, and next we came to the land of the lion-headed men."

Alexander was also said to have made a trip through the air in a basket pulled by six griffins. His method of steering his primitive flying machine was unusual. All he had to do was dangle a piece of liver from a spear held in front of their faces.

As recently as the eighteenth century, monsters were still big news. Early in the 1700s, a book appeared that described all manner of these creatures. It was called *The Travels of Sir John Mandeville*. Actually, parts of it had been around since the fourteenth century, since it had been one of the first books printed after the invention of modern printing. But in 1725 a new translation appeared and caught the fancy of educated Europeans.

Mandeville defined a monster as "a thing deformed against kind both of man or of beast or of anything else, and that is called a monster."

He believed that these creatures lived in Arabia, Ethiopia, or the mythical kingdom of Prester John.

Prester John was a legendary Christian king and high priest of India, and his story began with the appearance of a letter that he wrote to Manuel Comnenus, the Emperor of Byzantium, in 1165. This letter, which was really a fake, described his kingdom. And it intrigued the people of the day, since it provided them with

Prester John—the mythical priest-king of the Middle Ages.

a mythical kingdom in which all things, including monsters, could exist. Part of the letter went as follows:

> In our territories are found elephants, dromedaries, and camels, and almost every kind of beast that is under heaven. Honey flows in our land, and milk everywhere abounds. In one of our territories no poison can do harm and no noisy frog croaks, no scorpions are there, and no serpents creep through the grass. No venomous reptiles can exist there or use their deadly power.

It turned out that the writings of Prester John, like those of Sir John Mandeville, were hoaxes. Yet, for many different reasons, people wanted to believe these wild stories.

This book is about some of the weird and frightening beasts that have been a part of folklore for centuries. But here is a word of caution. Although none of these monsters has ever ex-

This is what some people think the Loch Ness monster looks like.

isted, don't be too quick to laugh at the people who believed in them. We live in modern times, but there are plenty of people who still believe in these creatures. How many people do you know who are sure that there are no such things as monsters? We don't usually believe in dragons or unicorns, but millions of people believe in the Sasquatch, the Abominable Snowman, and the Loch Ness Monster.

A memorial to Bigfoot. This is a statue of a Sasquatch carved in redwood in Willow Creek, California.

1

OLD TIME DRAGONS

One of the most famous man-eating monsters was called Grendel. He can be found in the old Anglo-Saxon legend of Beowulf, which dates back to the eighth century A.D.

Grendel may have been a dragon, or at least half-monster, half-man, but he is not described very well in the poem. He is referred to, however, as a scathing monster—a dark evildoer, with flaming eyes. This creature lived in Denmark, in a cave beneath a lake.

Grendel would come out from time to time

and act as a border raider, haunting the moors of the neighborhood. But he couldn't stand the music and the noise that came from the nearby Castle Heorot. So he decided to raid the place.

His first night raid into the castle netted him a feast. He killed thirty young Danes, tearing them apart, biting their bones, drinking their blood, even munching on their hands and feet. Those he could not eat he carried off to his lair.

For the next dozen years or so, this huge creature ambushed both old and young people. He would also eat the Danes who came to try to kill him. That was easy, since no sword could wound him. He even had the nerve to refuse to pay money to make up for the murders.

Beowulf, the hero, hearing about Grendel, offered his services to Hrothgar, the king of the castle. The offer was accepted and everyone went to bed, confident that Beowulf would protect them. Beowulf lay in wait, unarmed. He also had taken off his breastplate and helmet, knowing that Grendel could be killed only by sheer strength and agility.

Then into the castle came Grendel. When he got to Beowulf, the young hero clapped him in a wrestling grip. The fight went on for some time, and finally Grendel, trying to get away, had an accident. The result was that Grendel escaped, but he left one of his arms in Beowulf's grasp. Grendel never recovered from the wound. He died when he got back to his cave.

The happy Danes nailed the arm to the wall and procceded to celebrate. But the next night, Grendel's mother (who also is not described well in the poem) came into the hall looking for revenge. She grabbed Grendel's arm off the wall, killed a Danish nobleman, and carried both the arm and the body of the man to the underwater cave.

This time Beowulf put on his armor and his helmet and grabbed his trusty sword, which was called "Hrunting." With a few warriors, he tracked her to the lake, where they found the head of the dead Dane on the shore. Beowulf dived in and found the underwater cave.

Immediately Grendel's mother leaped on him, grabbing Beowulf with her huge claws. But the hero's armor protected him from her grasp, and he wasn't even hurt. Beowulf slashed at her with his sword and found that she could not be hurt by it. Then the wrestling match began, neither being able to hurt the other.

But nearby was Grendel's mother's sword, which she grabbed and used to try to kill Beowulf. His armor protected him again, and then he found another sword—a giant one, too heavy for most men to lift—in the cave. With this weapon he was able to cut her head off.

Beowulf knew this was truly a magic weapon. So he searched the cave, found the dead body of Grendel, and was able to cut his head off, too. But the wonderful sword melted like ice in the blood of that monster.

Then there is the story of King Lludd and the

Dragons were big in Norse mythology. This ancient
woodcut shows a struggle between one of them and the
Teutonic god Thor.

dragons. Lludd had built a city in southern England and, naturally, named it after himself. Later, the invading Roman troops were to change the name to Londinium, and still later the Saxons changed the name to London.

Everything was going well for Lludd and his subjects until what seemed to be a plague began to spread through the city. Men lost their strength. Women lost their children. Young people lost their senses. Animals and trees died.

Lludd went to France and asked the advice of one of the French kings, Llevelys, who happened to be Lludd's older brother. Llevelys told him that two dragons were fighting near Lludd's capital city, and that this battle was what was causing the plague. And the French king told Lludd how to get rid of the problem.

King Lludd went home, dug a pit in the center of his kingdom, and filled it with mead—an alcoholic drink made from fermented honey. The dragons fell into the pit and drank the mead, which made them fall asleep. The creatures were then put into two stone chests and buried in Wales. The plague disappeared in England, but no one knows what happened in Wales. We can only hope that the two dragons are still in their coffins.

Of all the monsters, dragons are the most varied in appearance. Some have four legs. Some, such as the wyvern (WYE-vern) with its barbed tail, have two. Some have no legs at all.

There are dragons with and without wings. There are dragons who spit fire and dragons who don't. Many of these creatures have forked tongues, pointed tails, crests on their heads, and scales on their bodies.

They can be smooth, feathered, or furred. But, basically, they are large, long, and reptilian, and they have nasty tempers.

There were land dragons, water dragons, and flying dragons. The most common dragons, however, were water creatures. That is, they lived in the seas, the rivers, the lakes,

Here is an old etching of a dragon that was supposedly seen in Chile. How many animals can you see represented in its form?

the streams, the rain clouds, or the water spouts. Even those dragons whose homes were in the dry deserts were said to live at the bottom of wells.

But the ancient dragons were more like

snakes with wings. The scaly fire-breathing types seem to be an invention of medieval times. Let's take a look at the early days of dragon beliefs.

About 1800 B.C., the Babylonians became the most powerful people in the Western world. Their goddess of the sea, Tiamat (TEE-ah-mat), was protected by a dragon. This creature had a

Is it a dragon or a sea serpent? It could be either, but it certainly is a little like a snake.

15

crown of flames, the head of a ram, the forelegs of a lion, a body with scales like a reptile's, and hind legs like those of an eagle. Merely to look at it was to die of fright.

Marduk (MAHR-dook), the chief god of the Babylonians, fought the dragon. When it opened its mouth to bite him, he drove the wind through the monster's mouth and into its body. This made the dragon puff up so much it could not close its mouth. Then Marduk shot an arrow down the throat of the dragon, which killed it.

According to the story, he then cut off its head. The next step was cutting the body in two. One half became the earth, and the other half became the heavens.

The Egyptians had a huge serpent, Apophius (ah-POH-fee-us), sometimes called Apep or Apop. He was described as either a human-shaped dragon or a crocodile-shaped demon.

His job was to attack the sun god every evening, causing night to fall. But every morning, he was defeated by the sun god, and a new day began.

The Egyptians thought up a way to give the sun god a hand at times. They thought that Apophius could be killed with a little magic. It went like this: Draw his image in green on a new sheet of papyrus. Make a wax figure of him with his name written on it in green. Then throw both the papyrus and the figure in the fire.

There were other dragon beliefs in ancient Egypt. People believed that after death the souls of the wicked would be destroyed by a fire-breathing dragon. These evil souls could also be eaten by a creature called the "Swallower of the West," which was a dragon that was a combination of a crocodile, a lion, and a hippopotamus.

Then the Greeks came up with a couple of new ideas about dragons. One of them was that a dragon needed a periodic sacrifice in order to prevent him from causing real trouble.

This sacrifice was usually a young girl, and if she were of royal blood, so much the better.

The other idea was that of planting dragons' teeth in the ground. Each tooth would sprout and become a full-grown human being, often a warrior.

Greek dragons had two other talents. Many of them could sleep with their eyes open. And many of them could see with their eyes shut.

The Romans had their dragons, of course. These creatures were thoroughly described in the *Historia Naturalis* of Pliny the Elder.

Pliny had great faith in the dragons of India. He wrote that these creatures were "of so enormous a size as easily to envelop the elephant with its folds and encircle them with its coils. The contest is equally fatal to both; the elephant, vanquished, falls to the earth, and by its weight crushes the dragon which is entwined around it."

Obviously, that was a fight that no one could win.

Pliny also said that Ethiopian dragons were smaller than the Indian variety, being only about thirty feet long. But they had the ability to twist together in groups of four or five and jump into the sea. With their heads erect, their bodies still entwined, they would set sail to some foreign shore where they could get more food.

So far, we have been talking about dragons that were merely monsters with bad tempers. But as the belief in dragons grew in Christian parts of the earth, they became more truly evil. To the early Christian, the dragon was a servant of the devil, or even the devil himself.

2
DRAGONS IN THE WESTERN WORLD

One of the most famous dragons of all was the one who was killed by St. George. It lived, according to legend, outside the city gates of Silene, in what is now Libya in North Africa. Silene, by the way, seems to be a popular place for monsters. It was there that Andromeda was chained to a rock by a sea monster, according to ancient Greek legend.

At any rate, the people of Silene were forced to feed several sheep to the dragon each day. After a time, the dragon was not satisfied with his diet. He demanded not only the sheep but a man to eat every day.

The natives went along with this for a while, but soon the dragon became dissatisfied again. He now wanted young girls for dinner. The maidens had to draw lots to see who would be the next victim. One day, the king's daughter, Sabra, was chosen.

As they were leading her off to her fate, a strange knight appeared on horseback. His name was George of Lydda, and he was on his way to see the Roman emperor Diocletian. Diocletian, a fourth-century ruler, was conducting a horrible persecution of the Christians, and George was on his way to plead for the lives of Christian slaves.

But our hero decided to take time out to dispose of the dragon. He made the sign of the cross with his sword and attacked the monster. When he wounded the beast, George told the princess to fasten her belt around the dragon's neck and lead it back to Silene.

The overjoyed people of the city awarded George the highest honors. And when he told them that he had been able to defeat the dragon because he was a Christian, they became Christians, too. Only then did George cut off the head of the dragon.

Depending on whose story you are reading, George either refused the hand of the princess or he married her and took her off to England.

The French version of the story of St. George is different. It seems that there was a beautiful woman who lived in the castle of Vaugrenans. But she apparently had no morals. She was changed into a basilisk (more about that monster later) and terrorized the countryside. Her son, a knight named George, realized that he would have to kill her. So he did.

George was sad over what he had done. He prayed to St. Michael and asked what should become of him. St. Michael said that he should be burned and his ashes thrown to the winds. This was done.

Dragons were everywhere in the ancient world. This
nineteenth-century woodcut shows a German knight
killing one of them.

But the ashes all fell in one heap. They were discovered by a young girl, who picked them up. Near the ashes, she found the Apple of Paradise and ate it.

After a time she gave birth to a son, and what a son he was. When he was baptized, he shouted, "I am called George, and I have been born on this earth for the second time."

Another popular English dragon came in the shape of a huge worm. It was the Lambton Worm, found by John de Lambton in the Wear River in northeastern England.

John had skipped church to go fishing. He hooked a giant worm and dragged it onto dry land. John was disgusted with the size and weight of the worm as well as the appearance of the thing. It had nine holes on either side of its mouth. So he threw it into a well.

The worm came back in a few weeks. It had gotten out of the well and was curled around a rock in the middle of the river. Every night it would go ashore, killing cattle and sheep. Nat-

If you saw something like this, would you call it a sea
serpent or one of those dragon-worms?

urally, it also terrified the people of the region.

John confessed what he had done and went
on one of the Crusades to the Holy Land as
penance. He returned seven years later only to
find that the worm was behaving worse than
ever. In addition to attacking the domestic animals, it was killing people, pulling up trees,

25

and drinking all the milk in the neighborhood.

John went for help to an old woman, the Wise Woman of Brugeford. She told him that he would be successful in killing the worm, but that there would be other conditions concerning his victory.

"Remember this," she said. "You must vow to kill the first being or person you meet as you recross the threshold of Lambton Hall. If you fail to do so, then none of the Lambtons for the next three-by-three generations will die in his bed."

John put on a special suit of armor and the battle began. After an hour or two, Lambton was able to kill the worm. Wearily, he headed home. Just before he entered the mansion, he sounded three notes on a bugle. That was a signal for the people inside the house to let out Boris, John's dog. Boris was to be the sacrifice. But nobody had explained this plan to John's father, Lord Lambton.

The old man ran out to hug his son. Not

The fire-breathing Dragon of Wantley, it was said, was actually kicked to death. Here is a woodcut showing the brave Yorkshire Knight, More of Warncliffe, doing the job.

wanting to kill his own father, John called for Boris and killed the dog. But Boris was not the first being or person that the knight had seen. The prediction came true, and the next nine heads of the house died violently.

But where did these dragons live? By and large, Western dragons were thought to be underground creatures. The only time they would appear on land was when they were lost. If they couldn't find their way back underground, they became angry and started killing anything or anybody that came their way.

Most dragons were afraid of nothing. But some of them were terrified of eagles. And others were worried about panthers' breath, because that could poison them. Still others were afraid of thunder.

As far as their diets were concerned, people and cattle were not the only things they liked. Some dragons would lie under trees for hours hoping to catch doves for dinner. Many were especially fond of drinking elephants' blood because it was supposed to be particularly cold and refreshing.

Besides the typical horrible sword fight, there were other ways to outwit a dragon. Some people said that dragons could be charmed by music. And there was a German dragon who could be conquered by tickling it under the chin.

Dragons could be used to benefit humans, of course. One of the most common ways of using a dragon was to have him guard a treasure. The idea of a dragon guarding treasure seems to have come from a Greek in the second century A.D. His name was Artemidorus, and he said that dragons could be found wherever treasures were hidden. He was a dream expert, and he said that to dream of a dragon was a sign of future riches.

There were Norse dragons who were evil beasts that guarded treasure from dwarfs, giants, and minor gods. There was the ancient German dragon, Fafnir (FAHF-ner), who lived in a cave and guarded treasure. He was killed by a folk hero, Siegfried, who took a bath in his blood and became invulnerable to all weapons.

Apparently there were a few dragons who could improve crops. Propertius, a Roman writer, described a ceremony in a town not too far from Rome. The town was protected by a dragon who had to be fed by a pure young woman.

The beautiful maiden was lowered in a basket into the slimy pit where he lived. Then she had to feed the dragon by hand without flinching as he ate from her fingers with great gulps.

If the girl were truly pure in heart, she would be returned safely. And this would mean that the crops of the town would grow well that year.

Parts of dragons could be used in magic. In addition to making a person invulnerable after a bath in it, dragon's blood, when drunk, could give a person the power to talk to birds. Also, a dragon's head buried beneath the threshold of a door would protect the house and ensure good fortune.

Dragons were useful to the medical profession, too. Here is a recipe to cure nightmares: Stir dried dragons' eyes in honey and drink the mixture.

The skin of various dragons will cure shivers.

Certain dragons can lick blind men's eyes to make them see again.

Even if the patient dies, dragons can come in handy. Ericthe, a witch in ancient Thessaly, was able to revive a dead man by treating his body with a brew made from a dragon.

So much for Western dragons. The people in the Far East had a different type.

This is a stone rubbing found in China around 100 B.C.
showing an Oriental dragon.

3

DRAGONS IN THE EASTERN WORLD

Early Christians thought of a dragon as an enemy. But the Chinese, by and large, thought of dragons as kind friends. The most important Chinese dragon, for example, the T'ien Lung, guards and supports the dwelling place of the gods.

The Chinese dragon is a mixture of several kinds of creatures. Here is a definition of a dragon from a Chinese dictionary published in 1600.

The dragon is . . . the largest of scaled creatures. Its head is like a camel's, its horns like a deer's, its eyes like a hare's, its ears like a bull's, its neck like a snake's, its belly like a frog's, its scales like a carp's, its claws like an eagle's, and its paws like a tiger's. Its scales number eighty-one, being nine by nine, the extreme odd lucky number. Its voice is like the beating of a gong. . . . When it breathes, the breath forms clouds, sometimes changing into rain, at other times into fire . . . it is fond of beautiful gems and jade. It is extremely fond of swallow's flesh; it dreads iron, the *mong* plant, the centipede . . . and silk dyed in five different colors. When rain is wanted a swallow should be offered; when floods are to be restrained, then iron; to stir up the dragon, the *mong* plant should be employed.

The description can be different, however. Other dragons were said to have triple-jointed bodies, camels' heads, stags' horns, cows' ears, snakes' necks, clams' bellies, fishes' scales, eagles' claws, and the soles of the feet of tigers.

Dragons were extremely important. Many believed that the law had been given to the Chinese by a dragon. There was also a legend that the art of painting had been introduced by a dragon.

Not all monsters of China were gentle. This one seems to
have set fire to a house.

The Chinese dragon passes along wealth and wisdom to men. It doesn't have wings; it doesn't have flaming breath; and it is usually quite small. Chinese dragons at times could shrink themselves and live in raindrops. But one Chinese emperor who laughed at a six-inch dragon found out that it could grow at a tremendous rate.

Besides swallows, some dragons were supposed to like elephant meat. They killed the huge beasts by dropping on them from trees.

There is a story about one that must have missed the elephant when it dropped from a tree. This dragon fell into the palace grounds of the Emperor Hwo sometime around 100 B.C. Perhaps it had been forced to the ground by a heavy shower. At any rate, it was dead, and a tasty soup was made out of it.

Japanese dragons were said to demand sacrifices. But, like the Chinese dragons, they could also start and stop the rains or calm the waters of the sea to protect fishermen.

4

MONSTERS ON THE LAND

The basilisk (BA-sill-isk), or cockatrice (COCK-ah-trees), is one of the strangest of all monsters that lived on land. It is also one of the most difficult to describe.

In the days of ancient Greece, it was thought to be merely a snake with a bright spot in the shape of a crown on its head. People in the Middle Ages imagined it as a four-legged rooster with a crown. It had yellow feathers, wings, and a snake's tail. This tail had either a hook or a rooster's head at the end. Centuries later, the basilisk was described as having eight legs and scales instead of feathers.

Many people thought that the basilisk carried a jewel in its head. It had red eyes, a pointed face, and a rooster's crest. The French version of the monster, called the vouivré (vooeev-RAY), was a reptile a yard or two long with only one eye, which was made out of a carbuncle, a precious stone. If you could steal its eye, you would be rich. But if you were caught stealing it, you would go insane.

The basilisk was supposed to be born in a most unusual way. First, a seven-year-old rooster had to lay an egg during the hottest weeks of the year. How a rooster was able to lay an egg is not explained. This egg would be round like a ball, and was pale yellow or blue in color, although it could be speckled. It had a leathery covering instead of a shell.

Then the egg had to be hatched by a toad. At this point the basilisk was ready to do its dirty work.

What could it do? First of all, it could kill a human just by looking at him or her. Its glance was so powerful that it could even kill itself if it looked at its reflection in a mirror.

Just hearing its hiss could cause hydrophobia (rabies) in humans. You could die if you even smelled one. It could kill shrubs by touching them and smash stones by breathing on them. Where a basilisk lived, the air was so poisonous that birds could not fly through it without dying. Fruit would rot for miles around the monster. It was such a horrible beast that there were people who thought that the devil came to the Garden of Eden in the shape of a basilisk.

There were ways of getting rid of it, however. You could keep a pet weasel, since that was the only animal that could kill the monster. But the weasel would die, too, after the fight.

Or, you could keep a pet rooster. If the basilisk heard a rooster crow, the monster would go into convulsions and die. Some people believed that if a human saw a basilisk before the basilisk saw the human, the monster would die.

If, in some way or other, a human got possession of a basilisk's body, it could come in handy. All that the human had to do was to burn the body. The ashes would keep away evil animals.

Another popular monster was the unicorn. This animal was not always thought of as being a one-horned horse. Depending on where they lived, people believed in one-horned oxen, rams, goats, bulls, antelopes, horses, snakes, and even fish.

Probably the first mention of a unicorn in the western world occurs in a book about India written by Ctesias, a Greek historian. This dates back to 398 B.C.

Pliny the Elder also had something to say about unicorns.

The Indians hunt . . . a very fierce animal . . . which has the head of the stag, the feet of the ele-

The idea of the unicorn may have been borrowed from the descriptions of the demon Amduscias. Here is an old drawing of him as a half-man, half-unicorn.

phant, and the tail of the bear, while the rest of the body is like that of the horse; it makes a deep lowing noise and has a single black horn which projects from the middle of its forehead, two cubits [three feet] in length. This animal, it is said, cannot be taken alive.

Most people did not believe that last sentence. Unicorns could not be captured by men, they thought, but a pure young girl could do the job. She must sit alone under a tree in a forest. The unicorn would then approach, lay its head in her lap, and fall asleep.

Some thought that only girls of noble birth could catch the unicorn. And even the noble girls had to be young, pretty, and slender. But there was one tale in which a young boy was dressed up as a girl and was able to tame one of these monsters.

Another method of catching a unicorn was to stand in front of a big tree and tease the beast. The unicorn would charge, and the hunter had to step aside at the last moment. The creature's horn would imbed itself in the tree, and the unicorn could not escape. Then its head was cut off.

Chinese unicorns were said to be gentle and peaceful, but the Western unicorn was fierce and untameable. It could kill elephants with a single thrust of its horn.

Some people thought that when the unicorn could not win a battle, it would jump off a high cliff and land at the bottom on its horn. The horn was so strong that the unicorn would not be hurt.

In addition to preventing poisoning in men, the unicorn's horn could be used by animals. Legends tell of animals waiting around a poisoned stream until a unicorn dipped its horn into the water. That act would make the water safe to drink. If a human drank from a unicorn's horn, he or she could run through huge fires without being burned.

Obviously, unicorns' horns were worth their weight in gold. They were stocked in medicine stores all over the world, although few people admitted that these were probably the tusks from the narwhal. The narwhal, a sea mammal, is a twenty-foot long relative of the whale. Male narwhals have an ivory tusk.

There was also a connection between the unicorn and the story of the Great Flood in the Bible. Some people believed that the unicorns all died in the flood and that nothing remained but their horns. Others thought that the unicorns were so large that Noah could not find room for two of them on the ark. So the unicorns had to swim for the duration of the entire flood, and they rested their horns against the ark when they got tired.

The centaurs were monsters with human heads, arms, and chests. But from there on down they had the bodies of horses. They were supposed to be wise yet savage at the same time. Those that lived in a country called Clyon ate men. The ancient Greeks thought of them also as fun-loving; however, there were stories that the Greeks' forefathers had not only be-

A drawing of a statue of a centaur.

friended the strange creatures but fought them as well.

The legend that tells how the centaurs began centers around a horrible man named Ixion. He had fallen in love with Hera, who was the wife of Zeus, the head god in Greek mythology. This did not please Zeus, of course, so he created a fake Hera out of some clouds. Ixion and this cloud-goddess produced a monster son, Centaurus. He was the first centaur.

Another story says that Chiron (KYE-ron) was the first centaur. He was born a Titan (a giant of enormous strength, but more about Titans later), the son of Chronus and an ocean nymph named Philyra. Chiron attacked the young Greek gods of Mount Olympus, but was defeated. The punishment given him by Apollo, the god of light and reason, was to make him a centaur.

For some reason Chiron turned to school-teaching. Several Greek heroes studied under him—Actaeon, Jason, Castor, Polydeuces, and Achilles, to name a few.

Chiron was killed by Hercules in an accident. By mistake, Hercules let slip a poisoned arrow and it hit the centaur. The end of the story is that Zeus put the image of Chiron in the sky, where it can still be seen as the constellation Sagittarius, the archer.

A medieval picture of a centaur with his bow ready, similar to Sagittarius.

The warfare between men and centaurs may have begun in Thessaly. The legend goes that a tribe of humans, the Lapiths, invited the centaurs to the wedding of their chief, Peirithous. Unfortunately, the centaurs could not hold their liquor and started to bother the Lapith women.

A fight started, the centaurs lost, and they were driven away. The days of friendship between humans and centaurs were over.

Here is a sort of reverse centaur, with a horse's head instead of a man's head. He is Orobas, the ancient demon who guards Hades.

In the western hemisphere, the Indians' belief in centaurs probably began when men on horseback appeared in lands where people had never seen a horse before. In 1698, such an event was described by Father Stanislaus Arlet, a missionary in Peru, when he and his party were first seen by the Canisian tribe of Indians:

> Having never before seen horses, or men resembling us in color and dress, the astonishment they showed at our first appearance among them was a very pleasing spectacle to us, the sight of us terrifying them to such a degree that the bows and arrows fell from their hand; imagining, as they afterwards owned, that the man, his hat, his clothes, and the horse he rode upon, composed but one animal.

But what about giant monsters? Typhon was supposed to be the largest monster ever, and he was one of a kind. It seems that the Greeks believed in two races of giants—the Gigantes and the Titans. The Titans, as we mentioned before, were giants of enormous strength who battled against the gods and ate humans. Titan wives gave birth to Gigantes, which had frightful faces and dragon tails, fifty heads, one hundred arms, and snakes for legs.

Zeus had imprisoned the Titans, and the Gigantes were angry about that. So, standing on the mountaintops, they started throwing rocks and firebrands up toward Mount Olympus, the place where the Greek gods lived.

According to the legend, the gods could do nothing about this revolt without the aid of a mortal. Hercules was elected to kill the biggest of the Gigantes, which he did. The rest of them either ran away or were killed by the gods.

Gaia, the earth spirit, was enraged at the gods because of this. So she gave birth to Typhon. His legs were snakes. His hundred-league long arms had countless snakes' heads instead of fingers. His ugly donkey's head could reach the stars. His wings could darken the sun. Fire flashed from his eyes. Flaming rocks came out of his mouth.

Typhon, on Gaia's orders, rushed toward Olympus. The gods were so frightened they ran away to Egypt.

Polyphemus, the Cyclops, one of the most famous of the
Titans, attacking Ulysses and his men.

51

Typhon's story is not over, however. He was partly responsible for creating one of the most complicated female monsters of all, the chimera, or chimaera (kye-MEH-rah).

The chimera was the offspring of Typhon and Echidna, who was half woman, half snake.

An Etruscan bronze of the Chimera.

The chimera was a combination of a lion, a goat, and a serpent. She was described as a lion at the front, a snake at the rear, and a goat in the middle. She also was able to breathe fire.

Another description of the chimera said that she had three heads, one from each animal. The middle head was that of a goat, and it was the one that breathed the fire. This monster, by the way, was able to predict volcanic eruptions.

Then there were the Greek satyrs. They were old men who had the legs, tail, and horns of a goat, but the rest of them was human. They were a sort of lower god and either lived in caves in the woods or under the ground. It was said that they ate raw vegetables.

Another monster was Cerberus (SER-ber-us), the three-headed dog that guarded the gates to Hades in Greek mythology. It had a vicious temper, a filthy black beard, a snake's tail, and clawed hands, which ripped at the souls of the dead.

Cerberus, the three-headed dog, as seen on a Greek vase from the sixth century B.C. On the right is Hercules, who tried to tame the creature.

The Parthians, a Middle Eastern tribe of the first century B.C., might have stolen the idea of the three-headed dog from the Greeks. Here is one getting ready to attack a Parthian god.

54

One of the most famous Greek legends concerns the hero, Theseus, and the minotaur (MIN-oh-tore), a half-human, half-bull monster.

The people who lived on the island of Crete in the old days worshipped the old bull god because they thought that their kings were his descendants. It had happened, they said, this way.

This picture of a sixth-century B.C. vase shows Theseus killing the Minotaur.

A Phoenician princess, Europa, was admired by the chief Greek god, Zeus. In the form of a white bull, Zeus carried her off and swam with her to Crete. One of the children born to the couple was a man named Minos. Minos became king of Crete. Later, his grandson, also named Minos, ruled the island.

Pasiphae, wife of this second Minos, also fell in love with a bull. The offspring of the couple was the minotaur. Minos had the minotaur imprisoned in a labyrinth, or giant maze, in the city of Cnossus.

At the time, Minos was able to demand a tribute from the Greek city of Athens. Every nine years he was given nine of the most handsome young men and nine of the most beautiful young women of Athens. They would be taken to Crete and sent into the labyrinth. Once inside, they were killed by the minotaur. Theseus, a young man of Athens, finally demanded to be sent to Crete. This hero was able to kill the monster.

5
MONSTERS IN THE AIR

One of the most gruesome flying monsters of all was a winged female creature of the ancient Greeks. She was the gorgon. There were three of them, all daughters of the ancient sea gods, Phorcys and Ceto.

The names of these strange sisters were Stheno ("the mighty"), Euryale ("the far-springer"), and Medusa ("the queen"). Stheno and Euryale were immortal, but Medusa was not. The gorgons were said to have lived on the Atlantic shores of Africa. And they had once been beautiful women, but they were turned into monsters because Medusa defiled the Temple of the Greek goddess Athena.

Perseus, the son of Zeus and Danae, was sent by King Polydectes of the Island of Seriphos to bring back the head of a gorgon. That meant Medusa's head, of course, since the other two could not be killed. The reason behind this command was that the king had fallen in love with Danae and wanted to get her son out of the way.

On the way to Africa, Perseus was helped by two nymphs who gave him the winged sandals of Hermes (the messenger of the gods), a large sack, and a cap that made him invisible. He was also given a large, curved sword with which to cut off Medusa's head.

When Perseus found the gorgons' lair, all three of them were sleeping. Their heads were covered with snakes instead of hair. Their hands were brass. They had tusks like those of wild boars. Their bodies were covered with scales. And they had wings.

Flying monsters come in all shapes and sizes, and
apparently use various methods of transportation.

One other thing. Any human who looked at
one directly would be turned to stone.

In order not to be turned to stone, Perseus
cut off Medusa's head while looking at her reflection in his shiny shield. As she died, a
flying horse sprang out of her head.

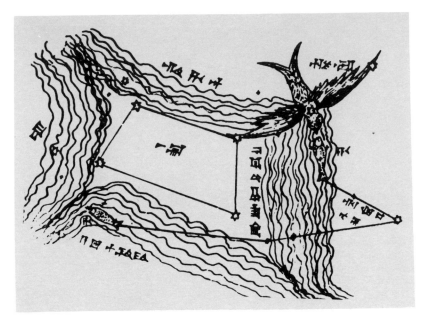

Pegasus, like the centaur Chiron, eventually became a constellation. Here is the great Square of Pegasus in the sky, enclosed by the Rivers of Paradise, the constellation Pisces. (*from an ancient Babylonian star chart*)

Perseus crammed the head in the sack and took off on the flying horse, with the other two gorgons chasing him. They did not catch him, but as he was flying through the air, drops of blood from the head fell to the ground and each drop turned into a snake.

When he returned home, he pulled out the head of Medusa for the king to see, being careful not to look at it himself. Polydectes and his followers were turned to stone.

Perhaps it was not necessary to go to so much trouble to kill a gorgon. There was another old belief that all one had to do was persuade her to bury her head in the sand. Then her head could be cut off.

The griffin or gryphon (GRIF-in) had the head and feet of an eagle, and the rest of its body was that of a lion. Some people said that it had four feet, others believed it had but two. Still others thought that its head had two horns. Its paws were red and its neck was blue. The female griffin also had the wings of an eagle, while the male had spikes instead of wings.

These creatures were enormous. They were described during Elizabethan times as having "a body greater than eight lyons and a stall [nest] worthier than a hundred eagles." It was said that griffin eggs had a capacity of two and one-half gallons.

Griffins were found in Egypt and Assyria, where their job was to guard the golden treasure of the sun. This was kept either in the griffin's nest or in a cave. One of the most obnoxious thieves it had to contend with was another kind of monster—the one-eyed Arimaspi (ahr-rim-AHS-pee).

The griffins hated men and they hated horses. But their biggest enemy was the lion.

Men who tried to eat the flesh of the griffin got terribly sick. But if a drinking cup were made from the claw of a griffin, it would change color if a poisoned liquid were poured into it, warning the owner not to drink it.

Even though the griffin hated horses, it seems that occasionally a female would mate with one. The offspring was called a hippogriff, and it had an eagle's head and claws, and could fly. But the rest of its body was like a horse's.

This old Sicilian mosaic shows a phoenix whose head is surrounded by fire.

The story of the phoenix (FEE-nicks) goes back to the eighth century B.C. The phoenix was a bird described by Pliny as being "as big as an eagle . . . as yellow and bright as gold about the neck . . . the rest of the body a deep red purple; the tail azure blue, intermingled with feathers of a rose color, with the head bravely adorned with a tuft and plume."

There were people who thought that it was

an all-purple bird, or perhaps part red, part gold. But they all agreed on one thing—the phoenix was immortal. It would commit suicide in a fire and then be reborn. That meant

Here is a phoenix about ready to burn up, as depicted in an early sixteenth-century manuscript.

there was never more than one phoenix at a time, and most people thought it was a male. But others believed that each generation was a different sex from the one before it.

There were different versions of how the bird monster committed suicide. It was supposed, in one account, to live in Arabia or India. Every five hundred years it would fly to the mountains of Lebanon to put sweet-smelling herbs on its wings. Then it would go to the Temple of the Sun in Heliopolis, where it would burn itself up.

The next day, a small worm would come out of the ashes of the bird. The worm took a day to turn into a baby bird. By the third day, the bird had turned into an adult phoenix, and it flew back to its own country.

There were other stories in which the phoenix lived for twelve thousand years instead of five hundred. It also might build itself a nest of spices in which to die. Then the new phoenix would carry the body of the dead former phoenix to the Temple of the Sun and burn it.

To us today, a harpy is a nagging, greedy hag. But to the ancient Greeks, harpies were female monsters. They were described as either winged women or birds (usually vultures) with pale human faces and human fingers with long, hooked claws.

They were the children of Neptune (the god of the sea) and Terra (the goddess of the earth).

A harpy apparently carrying off a victim, in an ancient Greek sculpture from the Tomb of the Harpies.

Harpies had a bad habit of screeching con-stantly. Besides that, they smelled terrible.

Their favorite sport was to swoop down on people and carry them off to unknown places. Sometimes they landed on dinner tables and carried off the food, leaving behind their hor-rible odor.

One nice thing: harpies could be kept away from the house if the owners touched the lin-tels of all the doors and the thresholds of the home with arbutus leaves.

The sphinx (SFINKS) was a popular mon-ster in ancient Greece and Egypt. The Greek sphinx had the head and breast of a woman, the body of a dog, the tail of a snake, the wings of an eagle, and the paws of a lion. Pliny said that she had brown hair, but everyone agreed that she had a human voice.

The sphinx lived in Thebes, where she ate the townsfolk and asked men a riddle. If the wrong answer was given, the guesser would be

The ancient Egyptians had
all kinds of bird-human
monsters.

eaten. If the riddle was correctly guessed, the smart young man would win the hand of Jocasta, the sister of the King of Thebes.

The riddle was: What animal walks on four legs in the morning, two at noon, and three in the evening? You can bet many young men died.

But then came the hero, Oedipus, who answered, "Man creeps on his hands and feet in infancy, at noon he walks erect, and in the evening of life requires the support of a staff." Oedipus won Jocasta, and the sphinx dashed her head against a rock and died.

So much for land monsters. Let's go to the seaside.

These flying monsters are not bird-people, but rather bat-
people. The artist Gustave Doré used them to populate the
underworld in this illustration from Dante's *Inferno*.

6
MONSTERS
IN THE WATER

Those who think that all mermaids looked and acted like the Little Mermaid in the Hans Christian Andersen story would be wrong. Mermaids (and mermen), of course, had bodies whose upper half was human and whose lower half was fishlike. But they may not have been all that beautiful.

Mermaids and mermen were said to have high and broad foreheads, small eyes, and large mouths. They also had flat noses, but no ears or chin. Their fingers were webbed, and

Some sea monsters were peaceful. (*from a nineteenth-century engraving*)

Some were ferocious. Here is a monster attacking a ship near Long Island in 1819.

Some sea monsters looked like giant squids or octopi.

An old engraving of a merman.

they had only four of them on each hand. Finally, some people believed that they had sharp green teeth.

Here is a description from Henry Hudson, the famous seventeenth-century English navigator:

> One of our company, looking overboard, saw a mermaid. From the navel upward, her back and breasts were like a woman's . . . her skin very white, and long hair hanging down behind, of color black. In her going down, they saw her tail, which was like the tail of a porpoise, speckled like a mackerel.

Some of them were not too gentle, either. They were said to eat human flesh. They captured sailors by singing to them. Then they would put their victims to sleep and devour them. Of course, there were humans who claimed to have eaten mermaids. It was said that their flesh tasted like pork.

Some people thought that mermaids and mermen lived beneath the sea in a kingdom of great riches. The mermaids were supposed to take their victims there and keep them prisoner. Indeed, many sailors thought that to see a mermaid was a sure sign of death.

Mermaid stories have been common to most of the seafaring nations. Even the Russians had a few. They said their mermaids were "tall, sad, and pale." But most of the stories come from the sailing nations of Western Europe.

Christopher Columbus reported seeing three mermaids off the coast of Guiana in South America on his first voyage.

Less than a century ago, in 1895, it was reported that mermaids came into the town of Milford Haven in Wales every week. They were there to shop on market day.

Early Christians believed that mermaids and mermen wanted to have a soul. The only way that they could get one was to promise to live on land and never return to the sea. Of course, the creature could not live very long after that.

Here's a story that is hard to believe. In 1403, a dike broke near Edam, Holland. A mermaid swam through the hole and was captured and

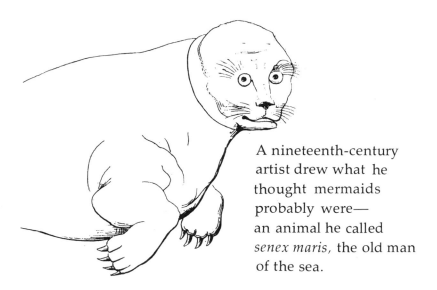

A nineteenth-century artist drew what he thought mermaids probably were— an animal he called *senex maris,* the old man of the sea.

taken to the city of Haarlem and made to work for a housewife. The woman even taught her to spin. The story goes on to say that the mermaid lived fifteen more years and, because she was so obedient, was given a Christian burial after she died.

Mermaids had talent, being born musicians. They sang sweetly and could play the harp, the pipes, the lyre, and the horn. Mermen, on the other hand, were great orators and could predict the future.

The bodies of these creatures could benefit humans, too. Mermaid ribs could cure hemorrhages. A bone from her head could cure gallstones, if you ground it up into a powder, mixed it with water, and drank it.

There have been hundreds of stories of other kinds of human fishes. In the Western world of the sixteenth century, these monsters were all over the place. A creature captured off the coast of Norway was said to look like a monk. Then a sea monster was found "in the habit of a bishop covered with scales."

In the last part of the sixteenth century, there was a written account of a sea serpent

with seven heades that was sent out of Turkey to Venice embalmed, which long after was made a present to Francis de Valoys, the French King, by whom for the rareness of it, was valued at 6000 ducats . . . nature hath never brought out a form any thing more marvellous amongst the monsters that ever were, for besides the fearfull figure of this serpent, there is yet a further consideration and regarde touchyng the faces, which both in view and judgement seem more human than brutal.

The monk fish. (*Pen-and-ink sketch by Virginia Aylesworth*)

The bishop fish. (*Pen-and-ink sketch by Virginia Aylesworth*)

The sixteenth-century serpent with seven heads. (*Pen-and-ink sketch by Virginia Aylesworth*)

Many people had their own ideas about what sea monsters looked like. Here is one from the sixteenth century. (*Pen-and-ink sketch by Virginia Aylesworth*)

Perhaps the most clever of the sea monsters was the serra. It had wings, the head of a lion and the tail of a fish. When it saw a ship it wanted to attack, it would fly toward it and hold its wings in such a way as to cut the wind off from the sails. When the boat was becalmed, the serra would swoop down and kill the sailors.

One of the largest of all sea monsters was the Scandinavian Kraken (KRAH-ken), also known as the kraxen, the krabben, or the sea kerven. It was supposed to be a mile and a half around and so long that it was sometimes mistaken for an island. Pliny wrote of such a monster being so big that it blocked ships from the entrance to the Straits of Gibraltar. Some people thought that there were only two Krakens in the oceans.

The monster was said to come to the surface only on summer days when there was a calm sea. But there were stories of ships sailing over a submerged Kraken. When the depth of the water went suddenly from six hundred to one

This sixteenth-century map of the North Sea shows a ship anchored to a Kraken. Notice the two sailors cooking a meal on its back.

hundred fifty feet, they knew a Kraken was at the bottom of the sea, and they were sailing over it. You can bet they changed direction promptly.

Fishermen, however, could be very fond of the Kraken. They thought that if the monster were at the bottom of the sea it would frighten the fish and drive them toward the nets.

The Kraken legend even fascinated the British poet, Alfred Lord Tennyson:

Below the thunders of the upper deep;
Far, far beneath in the abysmal sea
His ancient, dreamless, uninvaded sleep
The Kraken sleepeth.

Tritons were sea monsters. Here is an ancient Greek picture of Hercules wrestling one of them.

What could be a better way of taking leave of the monsters in the water than by mentioning everybody's favorite, the Creature from the Tiber? The Tiber is the river that flows through Rome, and in the fifteenth century a monster

The Creature from the Tiber. (*Pen-and-ink sketch by Virginia Aylesworth*)

was dragged from the waters. It was so bizarre that Polidorus, an Italian writer, was forced to describe it in this manner:

In the year 1496, was taken up out of the River Tyber, a monster having the tronke of the bodie of a man, the head of an Asse, one hand and arme like to a man, and the other of the fashion of an elephant's foote. He also had one of his feet like the foote of an eagle and the other like the hoofe of an oxe. The rest of his bodie with skales.

He also had growing out behind him, a heade olde and hairie, out of which came another heade of the forme of a Dragon.

It takes a glass of ale in his hand like a Christian, drinks it, and also plays at quarterstaff.

AT THE END

None of the monsters mentioned in this book has ever existed, of course. But there may have been reasons for superstitious people to believe in these creatures.

Perhaps, never having seen a man on horseback before, they thought he was a centaur.

Perhaps, after many months at sea, sailors' eyes would play tricks on them and they would confuse an island with a Kraken.

Perhaps humans have a deep-seated ancient memory of prehistoric animals, especially reptiles, and thus imagine that dragons really exist.

Perhaps, when people viewed an antelope from the side, it looked as if it had but one horn, and so it might appear to be a unicorn.

Perhaps a seal, a manatee, or a dugong, when seen beneath the surface of the sea, might look to be a mermaid.

There are countless other possibilities. But there are no real answers.

OTHER BOOKS
ABOUT MONSTERS

Allen, Judy, and Jeanne Griffiths. *The Book of the Dragon*. Secaucus, N.J.: Chartwell Books, Inc., 1979.

Anonymous. *The Travels of Sir John Mandeville*. New York: Dover Publications, Inc., 1964.

Aylesworth, Thomas G. *Werewolves and Other Monsters*. Reading, Mass.: Addison-Wesley Publishing Co., Inc., 1971.

Borges, Jorge Luis. *The Book of Imaginary Beings*. New York: Avon Books, 1969.

Clark, Anne. *Beasts and Bawdy*. New York: Taplinger Publishing Co., Inc., 1975.

Dickinson, Peter. *The Flight of Dragons*. New York: Harper & Row, Publishers, 1979.

Epstein, Perle. *Monsters*. Garden City, N.Y.: Doubleday & Co., Inc., 1973.

Hall, Angus. *Monsters and Mythic Beasts.* Garden City, N.Y.: Doubleday & Co., Inc., 1976.

Hamel, Frank. *Human Animals.* New Hyde Park, N.Y.: University Books, Inc., 1969.

Hill, Douglas, and Pat Williams. *The Supernatural.* New York: Hawthorn Books, Inc., 1965.

Hogarth, Peter, with Val Clery. *Dragons.* New York: The Viking Press, 1979.

Landsburg, Alan. *In Search of . . .* Garden City, N.Y.: Nelson Doubleday, Inc., 1978.

Ley, Willy. *Dawn of Zoology.* Englewood Cliffs, N.J.: Prentice-Hall, Inc., 1968.

Silverberg, Robert. *The Realm of Prester John.* Garden City, N.Y.: Doubleday & Co., Inc., 1972.

Spence, Lewis. *An Encyclopaedia of Occultism.* New Hyde Park, N.Y.: University Books, Inc., 1960.

Thompson, C. J. S. *The Mystery and Lore of Monsters.* New Hyde Park, N.Y.: University Books, Inc., 1968.

Trachtenberg, Joshua. *Jewish Magic and Superstition.* New York: Behrman's Jewish Book House, 1939.

Wedeck, Harry E. *A Treasury of Witchcraft.* New York: Philosophical Library, 1961.

White, T. H. *The Bestiary.* New York: Capricorn Books, 1960.

INDEX

Africa, 16–17, 19, 20–22, 57
Alexander the Great, 2
Andersen, Hans Christian, 70
Apophius, 16–17
Arimaspi, 62
Aristotle, 1, 2
Assyria, 62

Babylonians, 15–16
basilisk (cockatrice), 22, 37–40
belief in monsters,
    explanations for, 84–85
Beowulf, 7–10
Bible, 1, 44

centaurs, 44–49, 84
Centaurus, 46
Cerberus, 53

chimera, 52–53
China, 33–36
Chiron, 46
Christians, early, 19, 21, 22, 33,
    74, 83
Columbus, Christopher, 74
Creature from the Tiber, 82–83
Crete, 55–56

Denmark, 7–10
devil, 19, 39
dragon, 7–36, 84–85
   appearance, 13, 15–16, 18–
    19, 24, 34
   diet, 20–21, 28–29, 34
   Eastern, 33–36
   habitats, 13–14, 28
   old-time, 7–19

powers, 16, 18, 19, 34–36
religious beliefs about, 15–
17, 19, 22, 29, 33
uses of, 18, 29–31, 34
ways to kill, 9, 10, 12–13, 16,
17, 18, 22, 29
Western, 19–31

Egyptians, ancient, 16–17, 62,
67
England, 12–13, 24–28
Ethiopia, 3, 19

Fafnir, 29–30
fishes, human, 76
France, 12, 22–24

George, St., 20–24
Germany, 29
Gigantes, 49–50
gods, Babylonian, 15–16
Chinese, 33
Egyptian, 16–17
Greek, 46–47, 49–50, 55–56,
57–58
Greeks, ancient, 2, 17–18, 20,
29, 37, 44–56, 57–61, 66–68
Grendel, 7–10
griffin (gryphon), 2, 61–62

harpy, 66–67
Hercules, 47, 50
heroes, 7–10, 20–24, 30, 46–47,
55–56, 58–61, 68
hippogriff, 62
Historia Naturalis (Pliny), 2, 18

Holland, 74–75
Hudson, Henry, 73

India, 3, 18, 40
Indians, American, 49

John, Prester, 3–4
Japan, 36

Kraken, 79–81, 84

Lambton, John de, 24–28
Lambton Worm, 24–28
Lebanon, 65
legend, Anglo-Saxon, 7–13
Chinese, 34
Christian, 20–24
German, 29–30
sea, 70–81
Little Mermaid, the, 70
Lludd, King, 10–13

Macedonia, 2
magic, 10, 30
Marduk, 16
Medusa, 57–61
mermaids and mermen, 70–76
minotaur, 55–56
monsters
air, 57–69
giant, 49–52
land, 37–56
water, 70–83
Mount Olympus, 50

myths, Babylonian, 15–16
Egyptian, 16–17, 63
Greek, 20, 46–61, 66–67

Noah, 44
Norway, 29, 76

Oedipus, 68

Peru, 49
phoenix, 63–65
plague, 12–13
Pliny the Elder, 1, 2, 18, 40–42,
63, 67, 79
Polydectes, King, 58–61

religious beliefs about
monsters, 1, 15–17, 19, 22,
29, 46–47, 50, 53, 57, 62,
66–67, 74
riddle of the sphinx, 67–68
Romans, ancient, 2, 18, 30
Russia, 74

sacrifice, human, 8, 17–18, 21,
56, 67–68

sailors, 73, 74, 79
satyrs, 53
sea serpent, 76
serra, 79
Siegfried, 30
soul, 53, 74
sphinx, 67–68
suicide, 64–65

Tennyson, Alfred Lord, 81
Thebes, 67–68
Theseus, 55–56
Thessaly, 48
T'ien Lung, 33
Titans, 46, 49–50
Travels of Sir John Mandeville,
The, 3, 5
Typhon, 49–52

unicorn, 40–44

vouivré, 38

Wales, 13, 74

Zeus, 46–47, 56, 58